Milton
and His Modern Critics

LOGAN PEARSALL SMITH

ARCHON BOOKS
1967

Copyright 1941 by Logan Pearsall Smith
Reprinted 1967 with permission of
OXFORD UNIVERSITY PRESS
in an unaltered and unabridged edition

Library of Congress Catalog Card Number: 67-26655
Printed in the United States of America

"An interesting paper, or even book, might be written on Milton and his critics."

(RICHARD WATSON DIXON to GERARD MANLEY HOPKINS)

"Milton's dislodgment in the past decade, after his two centuries of predominance, was effected with remarkably little fuss."

(*Revaluation*, 1936, by F. L. LEWIS,
Cambridge University Lecturer in English)

MILTON AND HIS MODERN CRITICS

One

"MILTON," Mark Pattison said in his famous life of that poet, "is the first English writer who, possessing in the ancient models a standard of the effect which could be produced by choice of words, set himself to the conscious study of our native tongue with a firm faith in its as yet undeveloped powers."

This was for Milton an irresistible impulse, a vocation: from an early period he felt it to be a knightly, almost sacred calling. In a poem belonging to his nineteenth year, he declared his intention to write, not in Latin (as many wise people thought the wiser way), but in English, making his native tongue "search her coffers round" for appropriate words and phrases. Such was the controlling impulse of his later life; by his pen he determined to defend the cause of Religion, Liberty, and the Commonwealth; and even when blindness compelled him to lay down that weapon, he felt still convinced that he was des-

Milton and His Modern Critics

tined to compose by means of words something that the world would not willingly let die.

He was amply rewarded, not only by the acquisition of a vocabulary of invective which puts Billingsgate to shame, but by a whole treasure-trove of jewel-tinted words — of shell of pearl, so full of overtones, and arousing such echoes after echoes of association, that they have won him the enduring fame of the golden alchemist of our language.

> Fair silver-shafted Queen for ever chaste . . .

> All night the dreadless Angel unpursu'd . . .

> Nymphs and Shepherds, dance no more
>   By sandy *Ladons* Lillied banks . . .

>   In shadier Bower
> More sacred and sequesterd, though but feignd,
> *Pan* or *Silvanus* never slept, nor Nymph,
> Nor *Faunus* haunted.[1]

> Where the great vision of the guarded Mount
> Looks towards *Namancos* and *Bayona's* hold . . .

---

[1] John Bailey, in his excellent book *Milton*, in the Home University Library, describes these as "perhaps the loveliest lines in all *Paradise Lost*" (p. 112). He protests, however, very rightly, "that no fragment of a few lines can convey a full impression of the rhythmical, intellectual, imaginative unity of the Miltonic paragraph or section" (p. 183).

Milton and His Modern Critics

It would have seemed, but a few years ago, that no reputation was more firmly fixed in the heaven of poetry than that of the author of these and hundreds of other lines of equal beauty. The genius of Milton was indeed almost at once recognized. Dryden, though a Royalist and a Roman Catholic, was yet true to his art when he said (as is reported), "This man cuts us all out, and the ancients too." [2]

Even Dr. Johnson, who did not love the regicide poet, and whose phrase about *Lycidas* is almost too trite to allude to, — "its form is that of a pastoral, easy, vulgar, and therefore disgusting," — even this hostile critic is forced into an unwilling, but noble praise of Milton, whose "natural port is," he says, "gigantick loftiness," while of *Paradise Lost* he writes: "The characteristic of this poem is sublimity. . . . What other author ever soared so high, or sustained his flight so long?"

Writers of the nineteenth century were even

---

[2] Indeed, three years after Milton's death, Dryden wrote of *Paradise Lost* as "being undoubtedly one of the greatest, most noble and most sublime poems which either this age or nation has produced." (Preface to the *State of Innocence and Fall of Man*, an opera, 1677.)

Milton and His Modern Critics

more emphatic in their praise of Milton, who was regarded as being in a class apart, far above all those who had used the English language for poetical purposes. Landor said that *Paradise Lost* was "the noblest specimen in the world of eloquence, harmony and genius." Macaulay wrote without exaggeration that "by the general suffrage of the civilised world, his place had been assigned among the greatest masters" of the art of poetry. Time, Byron sang in *Don Juan*,

> Makes the word "Miltonic" mean Sublime.

"Milton's art is incomparable," Gerard Manley Hopkins wrote, "not only in English literature, but I should think, almost in any, equal, if not more than equal to the finest of Greek or Roman."

This chorus of laudation grew even louder in the first two decades of the present century, when it was combined with a greater effort to grasp the essence of Milton, and a more profound study of his age, his character, his influence, and the sources upon which he drew. A new conception was brought forward, especially abroad, of Milton as no mere Puritan poet, but as a figure of world importance — one of the greatest of poets, and most powerful artists of all time. M. Denis Saurat, who is the most eminent of French Miltonists, has compiled a bibliography of the books and essays written on the Continent and in America on this theme. It contains sixty items written before 1924 in America alone; of these M. Saurat considers as perhaps the most important single piece of work of the American group Edwin Greenlaw's essay, "Spencer's Influence on *Paradise Lost*," which he describes as "a decisive demonstration in favour of the new conception of Milton." [3]

All these Miltonists seem to take for granted, not only Milton's importance as a world poet, but the greatness and nobility of his character as well — all except a certain German, named Mutschmann, who tried to prove that Milton was not only an albino and a Neo-Stoic, but "a moral monster who had committed the most shameful offences and who was prevented by his cowardice alone from developing into a great criminal."

[3] Denis Saurat, *Milton, Man and Thinker* (1929), p. 345.

Two

ALL this was, however, but a storm in academic teacups; even the diabolic Mutschmann did nothing at all to injure the fame of him "whose soul," in Wordsworth's phrase, "was like a Star, and dwelt apart."

It was not till the end of the second decade of the present century that a serious attempt was made to dim that star. This renewed interest in Milton had no connection with the international movement I have just mentioned, whose effect was to enhance Milton's glory; it was a hostile movement, which, curiously enough, caused a certain perturbation in English academic circles. Its story is perhaps worth a note, especially for American readers, though there is no need to exaggerate its importance in the history of English taste.

The assault was launched in England, though not by assailants of English birth. Just when Milton's orb was tricking its beams abroad, and

Milton and His Modern Critics

the accustomed litany of drowsy praise was sounding from the chairs of all the professors of English literature, there disembarked on the shores of this island, one after the other, two adventurous young Americans from the Middle or further West of their vast country. The first of these Conquistadors to arrive had small academic standing; brought with him indeed little beyond an immense self-confidence in his own talents, and an equally immense contempt for those of other writers. He had as well a mission, a crusader's mission, which he came to proclaim to the large indifferent city he had crossed the seas to conquer.

His name was Ezra Pound. Though born as late as 1885, his birthplace, like that of Homer, is a matter of dispute: in *Who's Who* it is not named. I have seen Montana mentioned, and also Idaho. The state of Idaho has, I believe, the stronger claim. In 1908 he arrived in London at the age of twenty-three. There is a story — for though he is still alive, Ezra Pound has already become a semi-legendary figure — that this youngster from the Wild West made his first English appearance wearing a large cowboy

Milton and His Modern Critics

hat, and flourishing in his hand a cowboy whip, which he would crack to emphasize his remarks. This information came to me from his first English publisher, Elkin Mathews; but when, in my attempt to confirm it, I wrote to a friend of the poet's, I was told by my correspondent that he had never seen Pound in cowboy costume: when he first met him in 1911 he was dressed as a Regency buck.

However appareled, Pound, another of his friends tells us, came to London a complete stranger, without either literary patronage or financial means. Although few poets, we are informed, have undertaken the siege of London with so little backing, Pound soon attracted attention; editors gave favorable reviews to the little volume of verse entitled *Personae* which Elkin Mathews published. In the *Evening Standard* it was praised, and in the *Daily News;* Ezra Pound was described in *Punch* as "the new Montana (U.S.A.) poet, Mr. Ezekiel Ton, who is the most remarkable thing in poetry since Robert Browning." Back across the Atlantic the name resounded, and Pound was mentioned in the *Chicago News*, and the *Chicago Post*. All this more authentic information I derive from a pamphlet

Milton and His Modern Critics

entitled *Ezra Pound His Metric and Poetry*, which was published in New York in 1917. This pamphlet, though unsigned, was written by Mr. T. S. Eliot, who can be counted as the second of these crusaders. Mr. Eliot was also born in Western America, whither his grandfather had emigrated to the banks of the Mississippi River. He belonged by descent, however, to an intellectually aristocratic New England family, of which the famous President Eliot of Harvard was a distinguished member. T. S. Eliot was educated first at a school in his native city, St. Louis, afterwards at Milton School near Boston, and then at Harvard, where, after graduation, he was appointed assistant in Philosophy. In 1914 he was given a traveling Fellowship, which took him first to Germany and then to Oxford, where he spent the winter of 1914–1915 at Merton College. In 1915 he became a schoolmaster at Highgate, and in the following year accepted a position in Lloyd's Bank, which he occupied for nearly nine years. In 1927 he became a British subject.[1]

[1] For a full account of Mr. Eliot's career, see that admirable book of criticism, *The Achievement of T. S. Eliot*, by F. O. Matthiessen. Oxford University Press, 1935 (cheap edition, 1940).

Three

WHETHER Mr. Eliot and the slightly older Mr. Pound had made each other's acquaintance in America I do not know, but they soon became allies and collaborators in London.[1] Mr. Eliot certainly owes great obligations to Mr. Pound, which he has always been scrupulous to acknowledge. It is clear that in the years when he was first out of college, he derived a great stimulus from the older poet's enunciation of poetic theory; and that later many of his tastes and opinions first crystallized as a result of his close association with the author of *Personae*. His longest and most important poem, *The Waste Land*, seems, as several critics have pointed out, to be written in the form and style

[1] Many years later Mr. Eliot, when lecturing at Harvard University, told his audience that when he and Pound were working together on some journal which he does not name, but which may have been the *Little Review,* or Wyndham Lewis's *Blast*, they were mentioned, "by a writer in the *Morning Post*, as 'literary bolsheviks,' and described by Mr. Arthur Waugh as 'drunken helots.'" (*The Use of Poetry and the Use of Criticism,* 1933, p. 7: *n.*)

Milton and His Modern Critics

of the *Cantos* of Ezra Pound, to whom, as *il miglior fabbro*, it is dedicated. Like the *Cantos*, *The Waste Land* is loaded with learned references and interlarded with quotations,[2] and in addition to this form of a literary medley, Eliot seems to have caught from Pound that morbid preoccupation with squalor which "plays on the frayed nerves of modern intellectuals."

And yet this in many ways grotesque poem is a poem of real importance; we cannot pooh-pooh it away. Mr. Eliot has succeeded in what is perhaps the most difficult and important of all poetic achievements; he has created a new and personal rhythm, a choice and distinction in his use of words, which are all his own; and in spite of his meagre output, it is hardly an exaggeration to say, with the best of all living American critics, that "Eliot, in ten years' time, has left upon English poetry a mark more unmistakable than that of any other poet writing English."[3]

---

[2] Edmund Wilson says that this poem of only 403 lines includes "quotations from, allusions to, or imitations of, at least thirty-five different writers ... as well as several popular songs," and introduces "passages in six foreign languages, including Sanskrit." (Edmund Wilson, *Axel's Castle*, p. 110.)

[3] *Axel's Castle*, p. 111.

Milton and His Modern Critics

How enduring this mark will remain is a question for Posterity to decide. Certainly Antiquity (if I may be taken as its representative) can pretend to little voice in that decision. It may, however, be permissible to one who treads with aged steps the traditional paths of critical appreciation, adorned as they are with such a wealth of enduring masterpieces, to look upon this Pound and Eliot school of poetry [4] as being not unlike those other literary movements whose rise and fall he has witnessed in his own lifetime — fanatical enthusiasms accompanied by furious denunciations of those who are critical of such fervors. Such was the almost religious admiration, to take one instance, of George Meredith's poetry, which was a kind of gospel in my youth. This has been followed in more recent times by the cult of Paul

[4] The two have always remained closely connected. In 1928 Mr. Eliot published a selection of Mr. Pound's poems. This selection I have read: it contains much that is amusing, but nothing that to my ear sounds in the least like poetry — nothing comparable, for instance, to the beautiful, if incomprehensible lines with which one of Mr. Eliot's religious poems on *Ash Wednesday* opens: —

> Who walked between the violet and the violet
> Who walked between
> The various ranks of varied green
> Going in white and blue, in Mary's colour.

Milton and His Modern Critics

Valéry in France, and that of Gerard Manley Hopkins in England. But the course of literature is bordered here and there by conventicles of half-forgotten cults, whose chapels of malease are seldom visited now, though amid the rubbish of old papers heaped up in them the literary researcher may find perhaps fragments of poetry which possess the sudden, ecstatic loveliness we find in the poems of that lord of alcovists, and real master of Pound and Eliot — the enigmatic "black prince of wit," the squalid and divine poet, Donne.

But the verse of this modern school is after all not my concern: both Mr. Pound and Mr. Eliot have published prose volumes of what purports to be scholarly criticism; and Mr. Eliot, lecturing in America in 1933, described Ezra Pound not only as the most important English poet then alive, but also as a "very learned poet." [5] As to the importance of Mr. Pound's poetry, Posterity must be the judge. But with regard to scholarship, scholars are capable of passing an unquestionable verdict; and about Ezra Pound the opinion of all scholars is unanimous. He has published transla-

[5] *After Strange Gods* (1934), pp. 41-42.

tions from, or paraphrases of, Latin, Provençal, Chinese, and Japanese poems; but specialists in these subjects are apt, I have noted, to laugh when his name is mentioned. Latin scholars in especial have administered such remorseless castigations that one must almost envy the thickness of skin which has enabled their victims to survive them. But he who wields the whip had best learn himself to bear its lashes. One of them, for instance, has printed an essay called *The Discovery of Ezra Pound*, in which he collects a veritable snowstorm of "howlers" of which, he says, any schoolboy would be ashamed.[6]

[6] "The Discovery of Ezra Pound," by Martin Gilkes, in *English*, Vol. II, No. 8, 1938.

Four

MR. ELIOT's own scholarship is of a very different kind, and I find in his essays what seems to me some of the best and most penetrating criticism of recent years. Especially in his appreciations,[1] since by his disapprovals I am often completely baffled. In writing of Dryden and the literary critics of the seventeenth century he says "there is always a

---

[1] And yet by no means all his appreciations, as for instance the high value he seems to set on Joyce's later gibberish writing, and his saying "that Joyce is the greatest master of the English language since Milton." (Matthiessen, p. 135.) Nor can I in the least understand his immense admiration of the sermons of Lancelot Andrewes, in whose praise he has published a volume entitled *For Lancelot Andrewes*. These sermons rank, he says, "with the finest English prose of their time, of any time." I think I have read more seventeenth-century sermons than most people, but the preacher of whom I have never been able to read a page (nor have I ever met anyone who has been able either) is precisely this great divine. His *Devotions*, written in Greek, are of course quite another matter. I confess that I was pleased to read in Mr. Trevor-Roper's recent and brilliant *Life of Archbishop Laud* that he describes Lancelot Andrewes as preaching sermons of "unreadable preciosity," endlessly subdivided according to fixed rules, and expressed almost entirely through elaborate verbal conceits, principally in dead languages.

Milton and His Modern Critics

tendency to legislate rather than to inquire, to revise accepted laws, even to overturn" them. One cannot but feel that Mr. Eliot has himself yielded to the same temptations. When he remarks casually that the play of *Hamlet*, so far from being Shakespeare's masterpiece, "is most certainly an artistic failure"; that Goethe was no great success as a poet, and that he feels a distaste for Shelley's poetry, and finds his ideas repellent; that England "has produced a prodigious number of men of genius and comparatively few works of art," I am disconcerted and amazed. This way of writing has been described by one of Mr. Eliot's admirers as his famous "oblique" method of criticism — the quiet but deadly stabs, that is to say, which he gives to the established reputations of those whose example might be quoted to support conclusions contrary to his own.[2]

[2] *Stepping Heavenward* by Richard Aldington (Chatto & Windus, 1934), p. 29. In the slight disguise of the imaginary biography of a certain Jeremy Pratt Sybba, this book gives what seems a highly eulogistic (if now and then ironic) portrait of Mr. T. S. Eliot. Its hero is born, like Mr. Eliot, in the middle eighties at a town of the Middle West, and, early conscious of a distinguished New England ancestry, conceives the project of establishing himself as an authoritative critic. To London he

Milton and His Modern Critics

What Mr. F. L. Lucas has described as the "curious, cold insolence" of Mr. Eliot's enormous statements is a quality which Mr. Eliot and Mr. Pound share together, and they also share a common dislike for, and contempt of, Milton's poetry. This link between them (and a shared execration is a potent link) brings me back to the subject of this paper, the attempted disthronement of Milton. In 1888 Matthew Arnold, at the unveiling of a window in Westminster, had pontifically declared that "Milton, of all our English race, is by his diction and rhythm the one artist of the highest rank in the great style whom we have; this I take as requiring no discussion, this I take as certain."

But it almost seems that it was for the very

---

ultimately proceeds: and little by little, with cautious manoeuvres, and with the publication of little "exposure" essays, he comes to be regarded as the critic of critics, whom no one dares to criticize. The meagreness of Sybba's output is admitted; his support of the monarchy and the Anglo-Catholic Church is mentioned, and the fact that much of his time is spent in thoughtful gloom, probably of a religious nature. Our author rejects, however, with indignation the theory of certain critics who hold that all this can be explained by an inner unrelaxed constraint by which many Americans are afflicted. Mr. Aldington's book is largely a denouncement of these "constipationists," as he calls them.

Milton and His Modern Critics

purpose of discussing this point that these two young Westerners had crossed the Atlantic. As with the Titan of old who dethroned Uranus, it was the aim of one of them at least, it appears, to scale the skies and topple Milton from his place in the heaven of English literature. A fantastic undertaking surely, of which the most fantastic feature is the success, if only temporary and very partial, which has crowned it.

Belonging as I do to an older generation of expatriates from across the Atlantic, — the generation of Whistler and Sargent and Henry James, of Berenson and Santayana and Edith Wharton, — with all of whom I have been more or less well-acquainted, I have seldom met any of the flight of expatriates which succeeded ours; what I know about them is derived from books of reference, or from what is, I fear, but a partial reading of their verse or prose. Much of this writing seems to me fantastic, but I regard with admiration their adventure, which, just because it is so charmingly fantastic, seems to me what we should call in our native idiom "some adventure."

With Mr. Pound a loathing of Milton had early become almost an obsession; and in an essay

Milton and His Modern Critics

written, I believe, in 1918, but reprinted in a volume entitled *Make it New* (1934), he speaks of the personal active hatred of Milton, which he had already expressed in year-long diatribes, his disgust with all that he has to say, "his asinine bigotry, his beastly hebraism, the coarseness of his mentality."

Mr. Eliot is far too urbane to express his disapproval in such Miltonic terms; but he often hints at it in his quiet way — his "deft, inconspicuous sniping" as one of his admirers calls it. In his first volume of criticism, *The Sacred Wood*, when speaking, for instance, of the degeneration of blank verse from Shakespeare to Milton, he says that after the erection of the "Chinese wall of Milton," blank verse has suffered not only arrest but retrogression, and in his later publication, *John Dryden* (1932), he mentions Dryden as being "far below Shakespeare, and even below Milton." Mr. Pound shouted abuse, but Mr. Eliot's whispers proved more effective, somehow they carried weight, and before long certain professors of English literature began to tremble in their academic chairs. In addition to Mr. Eliot's deadly sniping (note the tiny drop of poison in the phrase quoted above, "*even* Milton"), what terrified the professors most was, I think, a theory he put forward (dark and difficult to understand) that in Milton there occurred a kind of disassociation of sensibility, a splitting up of the personality, which interrupted the progress of English poetry for a hundred years. This notion appears not infrequently in the pronouncements of almost all the Miltonoclasts. I confess frankly that I have never been able to grasp its meaning. But I have not been taught to think "in periods," nor do I find much evidence of the progress of art through this or that century. Whistler's dictum, "Art happens," seems to me about all one can say with any assurance on the subject.

Five

AMONG the first English writers to join the anti-Miltons was the well-known critic, Mr. Middleton Murry. In 1922 he published at the Oxford University Press a little book entitled *The Problem of Style*, in which small volume to my mind he singularly failed to solve this large problem. As a clue, however, to its solution, he quotes a chance remark from one of the letters of Keats, that *Paradise Lost* was a "corruption of the English language."[1] He omits, however, to mention that, not a month before, Keats had found *Paradise Lost* "every day a greater wonder," and that the later sentence was written in a momentary revulsion from the influence of Milton, which, when writing *Hyperion*, Keats had found too overpowering.

Robert Bridges in his essay on Keats (which is regarded by many as one of the finest pieces of literary criticism in our language) expresses his opinion that the best period of Keats's writing

[1] *The Problem of Style*, p. 109.

Milton and His Modern Critics

was when he fell under Milton's influence, and that in *Hyperion* "we are conscious at once of a new musical blank verse, a music both sweet and strong, alive with imagination and tenderness." [2]

All this, however, Mr. Middleton Murry ignores. "There is death in Milton," he reiterates, and writes, "I do not know whether he greatly enriched it [the English language] and I have felt many times in reading *Paradise Lost* and *Samson Agonistes* that he all but killed it."

The next recruit was Mr. Herbert Read. In 1928 he published a book on *English Prose Style*, in which there is, I believe, no attack on Milton. In his collected essays he says, however: "Milton did not think poetically, but merely expounded thought in verse; psychologically he was conscious all the time of a dualism, — on the one hand the thought to be expounded, and on the other side the poetic mould into which his thought had to be smelted." Mr. Read adds, however, "This distinction so briefly expressed may seem a trifle on which to dismiss so established a reputation as Milton's, and it must be admitted that the

[2] *A Critical Introduction to Keats* (Oxford University Press, 1929), p. 106.

Milton and His Modern Critics

whole matter needs careful analysis and consideration." In October 1930, in the organ of this group, the *Criterion* (edited by Mr. Eliot), he writes: "The critical conception of Milton is undergoing an almost complete transformation. In general the process is one of disintegration." Mr. Read goes on to repeat most of the charges brought by Mr. Eliot against Milton; that disassociation of sensibility which is mainly due to him, and from which English poetry has never recovered. He also repeats as a charge against Milton his use of foreign idioms — a charge which I shall refer to later. Mr. Read ends with the familiar statement that it was "the example of Milton that inhibited Keats and destroyed Wordsworth." Mr. Read was also appointed Clark Lecturer at Trinity College, Cambridge. It is curious how these Clark Lecturers all are apt to repeat each other, and how if an innovator starts, as did Mr. Eliot, a war against clichés, the enduring effect of his efforts is to enrich criticism with a new collection of them.

Six

The news of the threatened fall of Milton was brought by these lecturers and soon reached the seat of Milton's education, where the watchers of the Cambridge skies were prepared to witness this celestial catastrophe without, I believe, any very deep regret.

That son of Cambridge, Walter Raleigh, who in 1900 published a book about Milton of wise and beautiful appreciation, had long gone to occupy a chair at Oxford; and indeed, save for this one tribute, Cambridge had shown few signs of regard for the poet whom the world has come to consider her most illustrious son. As an undergraduate he had been given at Cambridge, from his singular personal grace and beauty, the derisive nickname of "The Lady of Christ's," and he is reported, some held falsely, to have undergone there the indignity of being flogged by his tutor ("whipt him," Aubrey says briefly in an added note). Milton himself tells us that he was sent away from Cambridge for a time, though he

Milton and His Modern Critics

was afterwards allowed to return and take his degree. Milton disliked Cambridge as much as Cambridge disliked Milton, and was apt to write — as three other Cambridge poets, Dryden and Gray and Wordsworth, wrote — in disparagement of that seat of learning. He loathed the College discipline and "the scraggy and thorny exercises of monkish and miserable sophistry," nor was he edified by the spectacle of so many young divines "writhing and unboning their clergy limbs" on the stage. Very differently did he write in his Ode to Rouse, Bodley's Librarian, of Oxford with its woods and its valley in which Apollo dwelt, "preferring it to Delos and the twin peaks of Parnassus." [1]

When, in the earlier part of the eighteenth century, Milton's fame had been universally established, his eidolon or image underwent at Cambridge a posthumous adventure, more grotesque surely than the shadow of any poet had ever before experienced. The most learned scholar of that university, and indeed the greatest scholar of his age, and perhaps of any age, the venerable, famous, and ferocious Richard Bentley, pre-

[1] *Milton*, E. M. W. Tillyard (1930), p. 171.

Milton and His Modern Critics

pared, at the suggestion of good Queen Caroline (in order that she and others unversed in Greek and Latin might enjoy Bentley's gift for emendation), a new edition of *Paradise Lost*, and published it in 1732 as a handsome quarto. The text of this poem, such was Bentley's belief, could not have come to us from the hand of a graduate of Cambridge; Cambridge must repair the wrong done to it by the half-educated editor who, after extensive mutilations and interpolations, had taken the blind poet's epic to the press. Bentley's episcopal biographer, James Monk, tells us that this scholar, having contracted an aversion to "the rapturous flights of genius and glowing language which distinguish the divine poem," had proceeded to remove all the presumed interpolations of the imagined editor.

This performance of Bentley's is so well-known that there is no need to say much about it. Perhaps the most famous of his triumphs is the emendation of the lines in Book I, describing the "Dungeon horrible" of Hell: —

> No light, but rather darkness visible
> Serv'd only to discover sights of woe.

Milton and His Modern Critics

Darkness visible, that can yet illuminate — a flat contradiction, Bentley exclaims. He suggests instead "a transpicuous gloom."

Even more brilliant is Bentley's rewriting of those last two lines of the epic, that quiet, dying fall with which the poem ends:—

> They hand in hand with wandring steps and slow,
> Through *Eden* took thir solitarie way.

Wandering steps? Bentley pertinently asks. Very improper, since in the line before we had been told that they had Providence for their guide. And why solitary, since they had no less than what they had always had, each other's company? Surely Milton should have written:—

Then hand in hand with *social* steps their way
Through Eden took, *with Heav'nly comfort cheer'd.*

Such a translation into English as she is spoke at Cambridge was too much, even for that son of Cambridge, Sir Walter Raleigh. He could find no answer to it: far too frail, he said, were the organs of human speech.

When Bentley comes on the lines in the Second Book describing the Hell-hounds which barked about the image of Sin,

Milton and His Modern Critics

> Farr less abhorrd then these
> Vex'd *Scylla* bathing in the Sea that parts
> *Calabria* from the hoarce *Trinacrian* shore:
> Nor uglier follow the Night-Hag, when call'd
> In secret, riding through the Air she comes
> Lur'd with the smell of infant blood, to dance
> With *Lapland* Witches, while the labouring Moon
> Eclipses at thir charms —

the Master of Trinity loses his temper completely. Let the editor, he exclaims, "take back his fabulous *Night-Hag*, his *Dance* of Lapland *witches*, and his *Smell of Infant Blood*, and not contaminate this most majestic Poem with trash, nor convey such idle, but dangerous Stories to his young and credulous Female Readers."

Seven

Modern Cambridge scholars are made, however, of even sterner stuff than the exasperated Bentley, and believe that the text of *Paradise Lost* comes to us just as it fell from Milton's lips.

Mr. Middleton Murry's war cry, "There is death in Milton," seems indeed to have echoed agreeably in Cambridge ears, and shortly after the publication of his book on *Style*, the authorities of Trinity College appointed him to be Clark Lecturer on Literature. But by the most serious thinkers of that university it was held that the revaluation of Milton, the discanonization and unconstellation of that poet, were due first and most of all to another Clark Lecturer, Mr. T. S. Eliot. Both Dr. Tillyard, the author of an earnest and useful book on Milton, and now Lecturer on English at Cambridge, and Dr. Leavis, also Lecturer on English there, are emphatic on this point, and before very long Mr. Eliot was given an Honorary Fellowship at Magdalene College.

Milton and His Modern Critics

I must say that I think it rather hard that no leaf of academic laurel is placed on the brow of Ezra Pound, who was the begetter of, or at least the first to proclaim, the "DOWN WITH MILTON!" doctrine (one falls into capital letters when writing of Ezra Pound from their frequent appearance in his writings). No Lectureship, no Fellowship, was bestowed upon him, indeed his name is never mentioned. Apparently it sounds somewhat harshly in academic ears.[1]

I must pause a moment to speak of three other Cambridge critics, Mr. Bonamy Dobrée, and Dr. Frank Leavis, and Mr. F. L. Lucas. Mr. Dobrée, who was born in 1891, is a graduate of Cambridge; with Mr. Herbert Read he edited that strange compilation, *The London Book of English Prose*. He shares the views about Milton of Mr. Pound, Mr. Eliot, and Mr. Read. "Milton," Sir Herbert Grierson quotes him as saying, "made the language stiff and tortuous, even distorted, unusable in that form by other poets, as Keats was to discover, but Dryden made it miraculously

---

[1] Edmund Wilson thinks that of this combination perhaps Eliot is too highly praised, and Pound, though he has deeply influenced a few, has been on the whole unfairly neglected. (*Axel's Castle*, p. 111.)

Milton and His Modern Critics

flexible. Milton may be the greater poet of the two, but in this respect *he injured our poetry*, while Dryden conferred upon it the greatest possible benefit."[2] How all these critics echo and repeat each other! Milton's supposed injury to the language as noted by Keats in a chance phrase of a momentary mood, the benefits bestowed upon it by Dryden, etc., etc.! Grierson is made a little impatient at hearing such parrot cries. He has, moreover, always disliked and distrusted, he says, this estimate of a poet by his influence upon others. In the first place the worth of a work of art is absolute and not relative. In the second, these judgments are very hard to make good, and as a matter of fact Dryden himself gained strength from his reading of Milton.

Could it not be as plausibly maintained that Milton, in spite of all his dull eighteenth-century imitators, whose epics and didactics hang, as Professor Oliver Elton has said, like a wall of felt between his age and ours, has conferred upon the poets who succeeded him a benefit far greater than the injury Mr. Eliot says he inflicted upon them? That his syntax, his diction, by enriching

[2] Grierson, *Milton and Wordsworth*, 1937, p. 122.

Milton and His Modern Critics

the poetry of Thomson and Gray and Cowper, and above all of Keats, was one source of the splendor of our great Romantic Movement?

But any such notions are far from the mind of the youngest and boldest of the Cambridge critics, Dr. Frank Leavis, who was born in 1895, elected a Fellow of Downing College in 1936, and appointed University Lecturer in English in the same year. He has already published six volumes of criticism, mostly, I believe, criticism of poetry. I cannot say that I have read them all, but from an essay of his, *Revaluation: Tradition and Development of English Poetry* (1936), I will take the liberty of quoting a sentence or two. Dr. Leavis says of the versification of *Paradise Lost* that a great deal "strikes one as being almost as mechanical as bricklaying"; and of *Samson Agonistes* that much of the verse is stiff and mechanical, and elegantly asks "how many cultivated adults" could honestly swear that they had read it through with enjoyment? He says cheerfully, however, that owing to four or five asides of Mr. Eliot, "Milton's dislodgement in the past decade, after his two centuries of predominance, was effected with remarkably little fuss."

Milton and His Modern Critics

We may smile at such pronouncements; but an uninterrupted tradition of detraction may do something to deprive great writers of their possible admirers, and, as Mr. F. L. Lucas says, distort the taste and enjoyment of many people. I have always regarded Mr. Lucas as the best and sanest of the younger Cambridge critics, and almost the only one of them who has some knowledge of the lovely art of writing. He seems, however, to have felt it necessary to throw an obligatory brick at the supreme master of that art, and writes of the "marmoreal stiffness" Milton imposed on English poetry, almost turning the blank verse of Hamlet to stone.[3] One feels tempted to quote to these pundits a passage from Landor's *Last Fruit off an Old Tree*, where he says, in his dialogue with Archdeacon Hare:—

It is amusing to observe the off-hand facility and intrepid assurance with which small writers attack the

---

[3] *Studies in French and English*, p. 232. "Milton's organ voice," he adds, "has no *vox humana*"; and elsewhere he confesses that he would gladly sacrifice all Milton's prose, were it necessary, for the sake of preserving Dorothy Osborne's letters (*Ibid.*, p. 172). Though I too love her letters, this preference for them to all the passages of Milton's glorious prose seems to me as grotesque as most of the pronouncements which Mr. Lucas has been at pains to collect from Mr. Eliot's writings.

greater, as small birds do, pursuing them the more vociferously the higher the flight. Milton stoopt and struck down two or three of these obstreperous chatterers, of which the feathers he scattered are all that remains; and these are curiosities.

Curiosities they are indeed, and I have sometimes wondered why, at Cambridge, though it was formerly a nest of poets, they should now bother themselves about poetry at all. Surely when Tennyson left the banks of the Cam, the Muses migrated to those of the Isis — to the company of Matthew Arnold and Swinburne and William Morris and Robert Bridges — while in the groves and Cambridge gardens the birds of song left almost empty their nests. "How ill that place," as Milton wrote to Diodati, "suits the votaries of Apollo!" [4]

[4] "Quàm male Phoebicolis convenit ille locus!" (*Elegia prima ad Carolum Diodatum.*)

Eight

'EN in our ashes live these wonted fires; and here I find myself railing at Cambridge as I was wont, when a crude undergraduate in my twenties, to rail at Oxford University. Even before that, when I was at Harvard the cry, "To Hell with Yale," seemed to me the apt expression of one of the profoundest truths about the University. I might have pleaded, on these occasions, my youth as an excuse for such tribal antagonisms; but such an excuse is hardly available at the somewhat maturer age of seventy-four. Surely it would be more becoming, and more profitable as well, to try to understand rather than merely to denounce this reaction against Milton. Group animosities and tribal war dances I find great fun, but I find in the serene interest of comprehension a more enduring pleasure.

Well, in the first place, Milton wasn't an amiable person. We may admire his courage, his devotion to his high calling, but there is little in

Milton and His Modern Critics

his character that can make us love him, as we can love almost all the great English poets. He was — as are many geniuses — an egotist; and like those other two lonely and sublime artists, Dante and Michelangelo, he was arrogant, haughty, and capable of inspiring the most intense repugnance.

> Soul awful — if the earth has ever lodged
> An awful soul

was the way his awed admirer, Wordsworth, described him in the *Prelude*.

Moreover the kind of poetry, the magical, evocative verse which brings tears to the eyes and gives us that shiver down the spine, which Housman has described as the effect of true poetry, is not what young people care for now; and the exquisite choice of diction it demands seems to them silly, or at the best a waste of time. What they seek for is "hard, positive subject matter," not beauty of expression.

Well, taste changes with the changing generations, and with the circumstances of which that taste is the almost inevitable product. I and my contemporaries were brought up in what we now see to have been a kind of Golden Age — one of those brief, rare halcyon interludes in the world's

Milton and His Modern Critics

history, when men could talk at their leisure, and read and re-read the books they liked. But now that the sun of our day is setting amid dark clouds, what comfort, with the prospect which faces them, can our successors derive from the thought of

> Hesperus, and his daughters three
> That sing about the golden tree?

And in the conflict which seems to lie before them, what auxiliary aid may they hope from the

> Knights of *Logres*, or of *Lyones*,
> *Lancelot* or *Pelleas*, or *Pellenore?*

The learned leisure, the labors of the file, the exquisite pains and pleasures of polishing their phrases, are the torment and privilege alone of those craft-conscious artists into whose pockets, as into the pockets of the well-endowed Milton, the world keeps on putting supplies of its negotiable coin. But these stores of old gold are almost exhausted now, and the necessity of writing for one's living blunts the appreciation of writing when it bears the mark of perfection. Quality disconcerts our hasty writers; they are ready to condemn it as preciosity and affectation. And if to them the musical and creative power of words conveys little meaning, how out of date and irrelevant must a poem like *Lycidas* seem to them, as it seemed to Dr. Johnson! It would not be generous to compare them to certain of Dryden's detractors, whom a lover of that poet described as being like "those crabbed-fac'd Maids who wished there were no such things as Beauty and Husbands because they have none."

Nine

PERFECTION, as that admirable critic, Swinburne, pointed out, is apt to be hated at its first appearance: it must be seen to be loved, and few have eyes to perceive it. To none but these few can it be acceptable at first, and only because they are the final legislators of opinion, the tacit and patient lawgivers of time, does it ever win acceptance. Now Milton from his earliest years had determined to seek for perfection; and for such an object, "hitherto unsought and undreamed of by English poets," he sacrificed everything, and achieved it. An objective of this nature, Dr. Mackail (from whom I am quoting) goes on to say, "will allow of no rival, and exacts prodigious payment. . . . Like the merchantman of the parable, he sold all he had to buy that one pearl."[1] Milton dwells apart with Virgil and Dante, in a kind of royal solitude; among the poets who followed after him, Pope

[1] J. W. Mackail, *The Springs of Helicon* (1909), pp. 147–48.

and Gray and Tennyson are the only English writers who never published anything till it was as perfect in phrasing as they could make it.

However, Mr. Middleton Murry tells us, a great work of literature is not so much a triumph of language as a victory over language; or, as Dr. Leavis has said of Milton, he "displays a feeling *for* words, rather than a capacity for feeling *through* them."² This thought (if it be a thought) places on a more plausible basis the modern distaste for Milton's poetry. I think I understand the notion (or do I?) — an earnest meaning, which blazes through the paltry words which almost fail to express it. This then, I say to myself, is style; style being, as Mr. Herbert Read has said, spontaneity — a perfect and prompt sincerity in the expressing of important meaning.

Mr. Eliot tells us that he found, in one of D. H. Lawrence's letters, an expression of what was the ideal before him as a poet. "The essence of poetry," Lawrence had written, "with us in this age of stark and unlovely actualities is a stark directness, without a shadow of a lie, or a shadow of deflection anywhere. . . . This stark, bare,

² Leavis, *Revaluation*, p. 50.

Milton and His Modern Critics

rocky directness of statement, this alone makes poetry today." The creation of poetry, Mr. Eliot believes, we are told, springs out of suffering, and is its expression.[3]

And yet the history of literature seems to show that the direct expression of suffering and true feeling is generally poor stuff. Nowhere, as Jowett tersely remarked, "is there more true feeling, and nowhere worse taste, than in a churchyard."

Milton's great dirge *Lycidas* has therefore puzzled critics who are of Mr. Eliot's way of thinking. *Lycidas* is generally admitted to be one of the most perfect pieces of pure literature in existence — the touchstone, as Tennyson said, of poetic taste.

Dr. Tillyard finds himself somewhat puzzled by this problem. Believing as he does that every great poem must have a true feeling behind it, he cannot but ask himself what is the feeling behind this lovely pastoral, with its rivers, its fountains, sheep, and pastures, and its sudden, irrelevant, savage, unprovoked attack on contemporary Bishops? Ostensibly written as a lament on the

[3] Matthiesson, pp. 89, 101.

death by drowning of a Fellow of Milton's college, Edward King, it was plainly not inspired by any deep grief at the loss of this reverend young gentleman.

Why, surely, Dr. Tillyard cries at last in triumph, it was the fear of drowning that gives *Lycidas* its profounder meaning! King had been with Milton at the same college; he too had written verse, and he too had sailed the sea, as Milton was about to sail it. Was not Milton in danger of completing the analogy by getting drowned himself?

One thing that I greatly admire in the Cambridge critics is their complete unawareness that such a trope as the *reductio ad absurdum* exists. I wish that, after proving hydrophobia to have been the inspiration of *Lycidas*, one of them would expound to us the significance of Oberon's speech, "Once I sat upon a promontory," or that of Coleridge's poem, *Kubla Khan*, or of the supremely beautiful last chapter of Ecclesiastes beginning, "Remember now thy Creator in the days of thy youth," for which a not very edifying explanation is usually provided.

Ten

Even more thought has been devoted in recent years to the meaning of *Paradise Lost;* to the problem of what the poem is really about, and what was Milton's state of mind when he wrote it. Earlier generations found no problem here; had not Milton stated plainly his purpose in the very opening lines of his epic? But, as Dr. Tillyard says, "such simple-mindedness can ill satisfy a generation which is sceptical of professed motives and which suspects the presence of others, either concealed or not realised by the author." [1]

Sir Herbert Grierson enumerates the various schools of thinkers, and their various and extremely divergent conclusions.[2] First of all there is the orthodox and "accepted" view, which practically began with Addison, and which Dr. Johnson accepted. According to this view, *Paradise Lost* is, with *Paradise Regained*, a rendering in

[1] Tillyard, p. 237.
[2] H. J. C. Grierson, *Cross Currents in English Literature of the Seventeenth Century*, pp. 251–63.

Milton and His Modern Critics

verse of the great doctrines of Christianity — the Fall of Man and his Redemption through his faith in Christ. This view, however, is contested by two schools of Christian thinkers, the Protestants alleging that the main doctrines of evangelical religion — humility, charity, Salvation through the Blood of our Saviour — are hardly mentioned in this poem. On the other hand those who reverence the Catholic tradition find that Milton draws little attention to the two great foundations of their faith, the Virgin Birth and the Crucifixion. Indeed the tragic figure of Christ crucified, which has won the heart and been the consolation of countless generations, finds little mention in this so-called Christian epic.[3]

Cardinal Newman describes both Milton and Gibbon as authors to whom good Catholics must feel a great repugnance. Great English authors, he admits, but each "breathing hatred to the Catholic Church in his own way, each a proud rebellious creature of God, each gifted with incomparable gifts."[4]

---

[3] "What overcame the world was what Saint Paul said he would always preach; Christ and him crucified. Therein was a new poetry, a new ideal, a new God." (Santayana, *Little Essays*, p. 61.)

[4] Quoted by Grierson in *Cross Currents*, p. 255.

Milton and His Modern Critics

With all this diversity of contradictory views about Milton's meaning, it has seemed necessary to have recourse to the modern theory of an unconscious Milton, who, without knowing it, wrote with a purpose very different from that of his conscious self.

As to what was the purpose of this unconscious Milton in what he regarded as his attempt to justify the ways of God to men, there are two main theories current, neither of which does him much credit among earnest students. According to one theory, Milton, though exquisitely susceptible to the charm of women, was — and perhaps owing to that very susceptibility — at heart a hater of these "fair Atheists," *Paradise Lost* being, with his pamphlets on divorce, a betrayal of his spite against his first wife for what he considered her cruel ill-treatment of him. According to this view, Paradise was lost when Adam was induced to partake of

> That crude Apple that diverted *Eve* . . .
> Against his better knowledge, not deceav'd,
> But fondly overcome with Femal charm.

These thinkers quote the perfectly uncalled-for outburst of Adam to Eve in Book X: —

Milton and His Modern Critics

> O why did God,
> Creator wise, that peopl'd highest Heav'n
> With Spirits Masculine, create at last
> This noveltie on Earth, this fair defect
> Of Nature, and not fill the World at once
> With Men as Angels without Feminine,
> Or find some other way to generate
> Mankind? This mischief had not then befall'n.

This mischief, due not only to the triviality of Eve's mind, but to the sensual folly of Adam, as he himself confesses — this yielding was the origin of Original Sin, and the triumph of Satan, who represents Passion, over Christ, that is to say Reason.

The moral therefore of *Paradise Lost,* as of *Samson Agonistes*, is that a husband must keep his wife in her proper place.

> Hee for God only, shee for God in him.

> Therefore Gods universal Law
> Gave to the man despotic power
> Over his female in due awe,
> Not from that right to depart an hour,
> Smile she or lowre.

Still more numerous is the Satanic school of Miltonists, who maintain that Satan, being an embodiment of the unconscious Milton, was the real hero of *Paradise Lost*. Satan possessed the obstinate pride, the undaunted courage, the heroic energy, which were a part of the nature of the regicide and rebel poet. Milton, Blake said, was of the party of the Devil without knowing it; a view in which Shelley enthusiastically concurred.

The Satan of *Paradise Regained* is very different from the figure of "faded splendour wan," yet regal port, which towers over us in the earlier epic,

> Like *Teneriff* or *Atlas* unremov'd.

He has become a polished diplomatist and a disputer about culture and morals, in place of a devil venturing all for empire and revenge.[5] And yet,

[5] If I may interpolate a notion of my own — at least I have not met it elsewhere — I should like to suggest that something of the Satan of *Paradise Lost* is to be found in Byron's favorite heroes, in *Childe Harold*, in *Cain*, in *Lara*, in the *Giaour* and *Manfred*. Most of these share with Satan a kind of Titanic self-assertion, still unconquered, still unreconciled, proud though in desolation like Childe Harold — and a high disdain from sense of injured merit, and secret woe, and though not unconscious of goodness, and "virtue in her shape how lovely," are doomed by some mysterious fate to pursue their own ruin and the ruin of those they love. Chateaubriand, however, claimed as sons of *René*, and therefore grandsons of his own, these Byronic heroes. But the origin of "Byronism" and the later influence of the Byronic ideal on all the literatures of

as Mr. W. Menzies has pointed out in his fine study, *Milton: the Last Poems*, the Satan of *Paradise Regained* retains much in his character, much of the conscious, or the unconscious Milton: "The fact is that Milton has put too much of himself into Satan's character, and cannot take it back at will."[6]

He is so magnificent a creation and is fashioned "out of such sound and true metal that he is proof against even his creator's own assaults." Nowhere is the conflict between the Puritan Milton who dictates moral strictures and the genius who so often speaks through Satan's mouth more strikingly apparent than in the great scene of Temptation in *Paradise Regained*, when the Enemy of Mankind points, from the "specular mount" on which he stands with Christ in Palestine, across the Aegean to "the eye of Greece," to Athens, and gives utterance to the most glowing, the most golden panegyric of the land of Attica; of the arts and eloquence and sublime poetry, of the

---

Europe have been the subject of almost innumerable studies, of which a brief list can be found in Professor Elton's *Survey of English Literature from 1780 to 1830*, Vol. II, pp. 419–20.

[6] *Essays and Studies by Members of the English Association*, Vol. XXIV (1939), p. 104.

Milton and His Modern Critics

civil wisdom and philosophy, which compose the world's immortal debt to the "old and elegant humanity of Greece." If this indeed be the real Milton speaking, may we not repeat in his praise, more truly than in the praise of any other modern member of our species, what Pindar sang of Peleus and Cadmus, that "though their lives had not been without disaster, yet the most perfect felicity attainable by mortals had been vouchsafed them, since each of them had heard the golden-filleted Muses singing, one on Mount Peleus, and the other at his wedding in Seven-Gated Thebes"?

Eleven

AND yet of these explanations of Milton's poems there seems to be no end. Thus, for instance, Dr. Gilbert Murray writes that his own feeling is "that, in the main, his imagined world is almost nothing to him but a place of beauty, a sanctuary and an escape." The most learned of our English Miltonists, Sir Herbert Grierson, quotes this sentence with qualified approval; he thinks that on the whole it is a true judgment, though, he adds, it puts Milton too completely into the school of Spenser (whom he had indeed declared to be his master) and into that also of the author of *The Earthly Paradise*.[1]

The latest, and to my mind the most commonsense, and at the same time the most profound of all the explanations of *Paradise Lost* comes, like our two young Crusaders, from the Western regions of the United States, but from one who speaks with a weight of authority much exceeding theirs. The voice is that of Professor Elmer Edgar

[1] *Cross Currents*, p. 262.

Milton and His Modern Critics

Stoll of the University of Minnesota, whom many regard as being, next to Sir Edmund Chambers, the greatest of living Shakespeare scholars. Professor Stoll has applied his sanity, his enlightened manly common sense, and also his great learning to this Miltonic problem, and, as with many Shakespeare problems, he has brushed aside much sophistication and academic cobweb. While admitting that the new German, Swedish, French, and older American investigators have added greatly to our knowledge of Milton's sources, he thinks that, led astray by the new psychology and by the craving for startling explanations, they have imagined an incredible Milton, a humanist son of the Renaissance, and of the civilization of Greece. They seem deliberately to close their eyes to the fact (though it stares them in the face) that Milton was a Puritan of the age of Cromwell, and (as far as is possible to a poet) more a Puritan than anything else. He literally believed in the Puritan interpretation of the Bible, he expounded in both poetry and prose the main Puritan doctrines. His Puritanism, Professor Stoll points out, instead of being modified by the growing liberalism of the times he lived in, is more and

Milton and His Modern Critics

more apparent in his successive poems. *Lycidas* is more Puritan than *L'Allegro*, *Paradise Lost* than *Lycidas*, *Paradise Regained* than *Paradise Lost*, and *Samson Agonistes* is the most Puritan of all his poems. In these three, as in *Comus*, the central situation is that of yielding to, or overcoming, temptation — and yet no notion is more opposed to Humanism and the Greek spirit than that of the glory of overcoming temptation or the sinful guilt of yielding to it.

But though he was a Puritan, and often seems a grim one, Milton was a man of deep humanity and above all a great artist, and his three great poems of Sin and Righteousness, Professor Stoll says, in his essay *Was Paradise Well Lost?*, all end in a quiet modulation, a note of reconciliation with life and human nature. "The grand style sinks into the simple, the music dies away on the slow chords of a cadence, the mighty pinions on which the poet was lifted in his flight float him gently down to earth again."[2]

They hand in hand with wandring steps and slow . . .

        Hee unobserv'd
Home to his Mothers house private return'd.

[2] E. E. Stoll, *Poets and Playwrights*, The University of Minnesota Press, Minneapolis, 1930, pp. 203, 249.

Milton and His Modern Critics

Nothing is here for tears, nothing to wail
Or knock the breast . . .

His servants he . . .
With peace and consolation hath dismist,
And calm of mind all passion spent.

Milton, who, Professor Stoll says, was "one of the most conscious, deliberate, unerring craftsmen who ever lived," deliberately planned and prepared for these magnanimous endings, these foreseen and necessary conclusions. In *Paradise Lost* his consistent purpose was to show how God brings good out of evil, and makes the superhuman life in Eden slope down by delicate gradation "to the level of life that men lead and always have led," "to human life as we know it, and as Milton knew it, of a mingled web, good and ill together, dim, sad but very dear." "Heaven and Hell give place to Earth; the exalted passions and unreal light or gloom of either yield to the twilight of human existence on this familiar earth."

As in the light of this interpretation I read again the last books of *Paradise Lost*, I find them suffused by a sunset glow, as beautiful in its mildness as the gloom and splendor of the earlier books. Michael's revelation to Adam of God's willingness to forgive is shown in His rainbow promise to Noah; the forecast of what life may still promise in "this transient World, the Race of time," and how the just may drop like ripe fruit to earth at last and fall, after a life of blameless joy, into

> A death like sleep,
> A gentle wafting to immortal Life. . . .

So compassionate is the great Archangel that our first parent began to wonder whether he should really repent the transgression he had committed, since God could so turn Evil to Good that its consequences might prove so much more good than evil.

"Nor love thy Life nor hate" is Michael's admonition to the human sinners, whom God had commanded him to dismiss from Paradise,

> Not disconsolate . . .
> Though sorrowing, yet in peace.

Twelve

But is this so great a conception of a great artist enough to shed the light of immortality, the

> Bright effluence of bright essence increate,

upon this poem? It is not. A poem may be wonderfully planned, rich with thought and variety of incident, but it must be poetry, or else it is less living than any other form of literature. Meaning, as Housman has said, is of the intellect, poetry isn't. Not the thing said makes poetry, but a way of saying it. It is vain to ask. Housman quotes Milton's line,

> Nymphs and Shepherds, dance no more —

"What is it in those six simple words," he asks, "that can draw tears, as I know it can, to the eyes of more readers than one?"[1] It is an essence, a spirit that escapes all analysis, Wordsworth's light that never was, *il tremolar della marina* that

---
[1] *The Name and Nature of Poetry*, p. 26.

Milton and His Modern Critics

Dante saw as he emerged at dawn from the Inferno. Useless therefore to seek in the architecture of Milton's great poem, or in the sources of his story, for the immortality of his poem. Nor in his thought; for Milton's mind was not that of a comprehensive great thinker; his pamphlets do not reveal any wide horizons of philosophic outlook. Nor in the materials of *Paradise Lost* do we find much that was not current in the common stock of European literature. The story of *Paradise Lost* had been told before him by Anglo-Saxon poets, by Swedes, Dutchmen, and Italians. But we do not read any of them; even the greatest of these, the Dutch Vondel, is not read, I am told, in Holland. We read Milton as we read Dante, for his literary value, not his thought. And anyhow, what the Muses think is of little interest; what we care for is what they sing.[2]

A wiser and more gentle soul than Milton, and a profounder thinker, was his younger contemporary, the Platonist Henry More, who entered Christ's College in the year before Milton left it,

---

[2] "Il ne faut pas demander à la lyre ce qu'elle pense, mais ce qu'elle chante." Chateaubriand, *Mémoires d'outre-tombe*, Livre IX.

Milton and His Modern Critics

and remained there all his life. He too was a poet, but his immense poems have been well described as among the most unreadable poems ever written. More was deprived of that mastery of verbal music, that inspired ordering of consonants and vowels, by means of which Milton, like his master, Spenser, flatters and charms our ears. Sound, which Pater said was more than half our thought, was to Milton a matter of supreme importance. Thus, for instance, the opening lines of *Lycidas*,

> Yet once more, O ye Laurels, and once more
> Ye Myrtles brown . . .

Swinburne described as being the most musical in all the known realms of verse; and who could be a better judge of the music of verse than Swinburne? If, indeed, as with some fragment of Greek verse, only these lines survived of Milton's poetry, would they not suffice to make his name immortal?

One of the most "serious charges" which Mr. Eliot brings against Milton is his devotion to, and expertness in, the art of music. These produced a weakness, Mr. Eliot says, of his visual imagina-

Milton and His Modern Critics

tion, whose sensuousness, such as it was, had been weakened by early book-learning, and produced also an undue devotion to the sounds of words.

All the arts together work at the common task of enriching man's life with beauty; and if Literature is, as sometimes happens, accused of leading astray her more sensuous and simple-minded sisters, Music and Painting, has she not at least learnt from them an added richness of pictorial or musical expression? If then Milton's long-drawn and richly echoing periods and paragraphs of verse, that bear all along in their superb undulation, are due in part at least to his musical experience, can we seriously regard this enrichment of his verse as the ground, as Mr. Eliot would have it, of a charge against him?

Thirteen

MILTON's love of words, simply for their sound and their associations, is shown by the abundance, the almost super-abundance, of the names of places or people in his verse. These "muster-rolls of names," as Macaulay pointed out in one of the rare passages of delicate literary appreciation to be found in his essays, "are not always more appropriate or more melodious than other names. But they are charmed names."

Like the dwelling-place of our infancy revisited in manhood, like the song of our country heard in a strange land, they produce upon us an effect wholly independent of their intrinsic value. One transports us back to a remote period of history. Another places us among the novel scenes and manners of a distant region. A third evokes all the dear classical recollections of childhood, the school-room, the dog-eared Virgil, the holiday, and the prize. A fourth brings before us the splendid phantoms of chivalrous romance, the trophied lists, the embroidered housings, the quaint devices, the haunted forests, the enchanted gardens, the achievements of enamoured knights, and the smiles of rescued princesses.

Milton and His Modern Critics

How reviving it is to find a son of Cambridge splashing the purple ink about in so genial and lavish a fashion!

More true to his alma mater was the Master of Macaulay's college who trod with his heavy foot in no haunted forests, nor had the least truck with enchanted princesses. Richard Bentley loved money, but it was English sterling he loved, not

> The wealth of *Ormus* and of *Ind,*
> Or where the gorgeous East with richest hand
> Show'rs on her Kings *barbaric* Pearl and Gold.

When Bentley came on names like *Babilon*, or great *Alcairo*, *Aspramont* or *Montalban*, *Damasco* or *Marocco* or *Trebisond*, these names, he declared, were plainly foisted into the text by the perfidious editor, "since Milton had too much judgment to sully his Poem with such romantic Trash."

But Milton not only loved such names, he loved also the adjectives formed from them, from the names of gods and rivers and lands and cities and mountains: *Plutonian, Titanian, Circean, Pegasean, Gorgonian, Stygian, Arcadian, Elysian,*

Milton and His Modern Critics
Hesperian, Babylonian, Olympian, Atlantean,
are a few examples of these nominal adjectives in which some critics find so little beauty, and Milton found so much.

Fourteen

"MILTON," says Sir Herbert Grierson, "is of the same caste as Spenser and Dante and Virgil and the Greek tragedians, the poets who are not content to confine themselves too rigidly to a 'language such as men do use,' but claim for the poet the liberty to build for himself a statelier speech, to move in brocaded garments."[1]

He felt himself perfectly at liberty to lay tribute on all the possible resources of the nation's linguistic coffers, from old archaic words to the new words he created for himself out of the rags and fragments he found in their recesses. For Milton often coined the words he wanted, and the Oxford Dictionary finds in his writings the first appearance of many words which are now familiar to us all. They may possibly have been used before, yet, like the coins of a great king, they seem to bear his image stamped upon them — *dimensionless, infinitude, emblazonry, liturgical,*

[1] *Cross Currents*, p. 242.

Milton and His Modern Critics

bannered, ensanguined, horrent, anarch, Satanic, echoing, irradiance, pandemonium.

As a creator also of compound epithets Milton ranks with the two other greatest of our lords of language, with his master, Spenser, and with Shakespeare. Among an almost countless number of such epithets Mr. Bernard Groom[2] mentions "*smooth-shaven* Green," "*wide-water'd* shoar," "branching elm *star-proof*," "*vermeil-tinctured* lip," "*rushy-fringed* bank," the "*deep-vaulted* den" of Hell and the nightingale's "*thick-warbl'd* notes." Many of these epithets, Mr. Groom says, are frankly decorative, and reveal alike the sensuous and the imaginative sides of Milton's nature.

Milton, who was, Mr. Groom says, "the most deliberate and calculating student of verbal effects who had yet appeared in England," would often take from the current usage some accustomed word, and restore what is called in numismatics its "erudition," the finish and clear-cut workmanship to such a coin of speech, made trite by usage.

Thus Milton describes as a "*secular* bird" the Phoenix, born once in a hundred years; and as an

[2] S. P. E. Tract XLIX, p. 305.

Milton and His Modern Critics

"*enormous* bliss" the scents of the Paradisal garden. So also the moon unveiling from amid clouds, "*apparent* Queen," her peerless light, and Satan asks who shall traverse from Hell to earth the dark abyss of space,

> And through the *palpable obscure* find out
> His *uncouth* way

to "this *opacious* Earth," "this *punctual* spot."

But the inhabitants of Heaven seem even more addicted than those of Hell to this pedantry. Thus the Archangel Raphael speaks of the "*parcimonious* Emmet," of the sun rising on the *enlighten'd* Earth, and of *obsequious* Night following the end of day, and *inducing* Darkness on earth. Even the Founder of our Faith does not disdain this kind of exquisite punning, as when for instance he described himself as *illustrated* by the hatred of his enemies.

Mark Pattison writes that only "by diligent practice and incessant exercise of attention and care, could Milton have educated his sensibility to the specific power of words, to the nicety which he attained beyond any other of our

Milton and His Modern Critics

poets," and the enjoyment of which is the last reward of consummate scholarship.[3]

---

[3] Milton's art is so consummate, John Bailey says, that there is much that escapes analysis, though certain elements can be noted. Among them he mentions Milton's use of monosyllables to express the solemnity of grave crisis or deep emotion, as in the line

> So clomb this first grand Thief into Gods Fould,

where these tremendous monosyllables, like a bell tolling in the silence of midnight, force our attention on the doom of the world that took its beginning when Satan entered Paradise. So also when Eve took the fatal apple,

> She pluck'd, she eat:
> Earth felt the wound, and Nature from her seat
> Sighing through all her Works gave signs of woe,
> That all was lost.

— *Milton*, John Bailey, pp. 166–67, 210

Fifteen

OF his scholarship Milton made still another use in borrowing from the classics a syntax of his own. This shocked Dr. Johnson, guilty though he was himself of the same transgression. Milton, he wrote, "was desirous to use English words with a foreign idiom. . . . Of him, at last, may be said, what Jonson says of Spenser, that he *wrote no language*, but has formed what Butler calls a *Babylonish Dialect*, in itself harsh and barbarous, but made by exalted genius, and extensive learning, the vehicle of so much instruction and so much pleasure, that, like other lovers, we find grace in its deformity."

This charge is repeated over and over again, without Dr. Johnson's qualifications, by those who write in disparagement of Milton, from Ezra Pound to the Cambridge critics, Dr. Leavis and Mr. Bonamy Dobrée. It is indeed what they consider the weightiest of the charges against Milton. When Mr. Eliot speaks out explicitly at last in

Milton and His Modern Critics

a volume edited by Herbert Read[1] and brings, in a little eight-paged "exposure" essay on the *Verse of John Milton*, several charges against that poet, one of them is "in respect to the deterioration — the peculiar kind of deterioration — to which he subjected the language." An element of this deterioration is Milton's involved syntax which he compares to its disadvantage with the development of Joyce's gibberish in his great *Work in Progress*. Mr. Eliot admits, it would seem reluctantly, that Milton is a great poet, but, he adds, "it is something of a puzzle to decide in what his greatness consists. On analysis, the marks against him appear both more numerous and more significant than the marks to his credit. . . . His misdeeds as a poet have been called attention to, as by Mr. Ezra Pound, but usually in passing." "Milton is unsatisfactory," seems to be Mr. Eliot's general conclusion.

For more old-fashioned persons, who do not wish "to put the fool upon all mankind," but who, retaining a certain respect for long-estab-

[1] *Essays and Studies by Members of the English Association*, Vol. XXI (1936), pp. 32–40.

Milton and His Modern Critics

lished reputations, prefer not to live in a world of statues toppling beneath a sky of falling stars, it may be worth while to point out that what seems to be the gist of the case against Milton, that of the character of his syntax, has been answered (if it need an answer) by the finest craftsman who has handled English since the time of Milton, by Robert Bridges (whose name, by the way, the disparagers of Milton do not so much as deign to mention). In his essay on Keats, Bridges says that the inversion which Keats learned to practise from Milton's example is "of the essence of good style. In ordinary speech the words follow a common order prescribed by use . . . but the first thing that a writer must do is to get his words in the order of his ideas, as he wishes them to enter the reader's mind; and when such an arrangement happens not to be the order of common speech, it may be called a grammatical inversion. To take the simplest case, the position of the adjective with regard to its substantive: in French it generally follows the substantive, and this is in most cases its proper place, and for this reason alone descrip-

Milton and His Modern Critics

tions of scenery are generally more pictorial in French prose than in English, the necessarily frequent predicates being in their natural position; in English the common use sets the epithet before the object, and when this is a malposition of ideas, a poet must invert either his grammar or his ideas."[2] (As an illustration of this beauty of inversion we may compare Milton's "darkness visible," a Rembrandtesque phrase which is superior in its beauty to my mind, to "visible darkness" — or even to Bentley's famous "transpicuous gloom.")

In writing of the transposition of adjectives which produce grammatical inversions, Bridges said that what was true of adjectives was true of every word in the sentence. The damage done to our speech by our loss of inflections has, in spite of its immense advantages in perspicuity and ease, been more than once noticed; and attention has been called to delicate and innumerable beauties which Greek and Latin writers (especially Latin) can create by the subtle placing

[2] *Collected Essays, Papers, etc., of Robert Bridges*, IV, "A Critical Introduction to Keats" (1929), pp. 108–09.

Milton and His Modern Critics

of their words. Robert Bridges illustrates this beauty, this graceful variety of syntax, which is forbidden to us, by an example from the second collect at Evening Prayer in our Prayer Book — "Give unto Thy servants that peace which the world cannot give." This is a translation, he says, of the Latin *da servis tuis illam quam mundus dare non potest pacem*. "The English is good," Bridges adds, "but the artistic order of the Latin words, which in English would be an unintelligible disorder, assists and enforces the meaning without the slightest obscurity, and the words group themselves in a sort of dance figure, instead of a 'march past.' "[3]

Now this cast-iron word order which most of us are forced to use to express our meaning Milton deliberately broke now and then, to give variety to his syntax. Examples of a bold use of classical idiom will be found, for instance, in the lines,

> That Shepherd who first taught the chosen Seed
> *In the Beginning* how the Heav'ns and Earth
> Rose out of *Chaos* . . .

[3] S. P. E. Tract IX, p. 20.

Milton and His Modern Critics

>That Sea-beast
>*Leviathan*, which God of all his works
>*Created hugest* that swim the Ocean stream —
>
>*Bacchus* that first from out the purple Grape,
>Crush't the sweet poyson of mis-used Wine
>After the *Tuscan* Mariners transform'd
>Coasting the *Tyrrhene* shore, as the winds listed,
>On *Circes* Iland fell (who knows not *Circe*
>The daughter of the Sun? Whose charmed Cup
>Whoever tasted, lost his upright shape,
>And downward fell into a groveling Swine). . . .

Milton, Addison wrote, raised his language by the borrowing of foreign idiom. All of us have learned to love the vivacity of those idioms of Anglo-Irish speech — "I took the hand of her," "Is herself at home?", "He interrupted me, and I writing my letters" — which are simply translations into English of idioms which are perfectly correct in Irish.

Indeed, how anyone with the least historical knowledge of that exquisite amalgam and shimmering mosaic of Anglo-Saxon, Danish, Greek and Latin, Dutch and French words and idioms which make our language — the speech of Shakespeare — the most composite, varied, eloquent, and in many ways the most beautiful form of human utterance can bring as a grave charge against Milton his attempt to make it by his borrowings still richer and more sublime — such a charge as this is something which may well amaze the philologer. Milton, moreover, while enriching with foreign idioms our uninflected speech, is yet careful to preserve and give emphasis to those inflections which we still preserve.

> Him the Almighty Power
> Hurld headlong flaming from th' Etherial Skie . . .
>
> Him haply slumbring on the *Norway* foam . . .
>
> Whom thus the meager Shadow answerd soon —

In one of the supreme scenes of *Paradise Lost*, the scene of the Temptation and the Fall, Adam says to Eve after this disaster,

> Mee first
> He ruin'd, now Mankind; whom will he next?

In the lines,

> Me miserable! which way shall I flie
> Infinite wrauth, and infinite despaire?

Milton and His Modern Critics

Milton indulges in the double pleasure of borrowing a Latin idiom (*me miserum*) and of using the personal pronoun in the inflected form.[4]

[4] Mr. A. W. Verity, in his admirable edition of *Paradise Lost* (Cambridge University Press, 1910), states that in the phrase "us dispossest" (VII, 142) Milton meant the pronoun to be the dative, "as suggesting the Latin ablative absolute more than the nominative absolute does." Thus, "*me* overthrown" (in *S. A.* 463) has more of a Latin sound than "*I* overthrown." Mr. Verity gives in his notes hundreds of examples of Milton's borrowing of Greek and Latin idioms.

Sixteen

BORED as one may well be by all the talk about Milton's spiritual message, or by all the explanations in accordance with the new psychology of his unconscious meaning, it is certainly a temptation to treat this great Puritan epic merely as a verbal achievement — an odd amazing episode in the history of the English language. To one who is above all a vocabularist the temptation is all the stronger to explain the magic of this magician (as far as it is capable of explanation) by the words he used; and since it is undoubtedly from the potency of these words that, in spite of the remoteness of its subject, *Paradise Lost* still survives, while all other religious epics are forgotten, how can one help regarding Milton in the way Carlyle is now coming to be regarded, as a writer who had filled his memory and imagination with sounding vocables, which at last burst out, not only, as with Carlyle, in glorious invective, but with the incomparable music of Milton's lovely song as well?

Milton and His Modern Critics

To take one instance of the miracles which he performs with words, let us watch him touch with his enchanting wand of style that object to be found in most old-fashioned houses, the nuptial couch. In hymning the familiar theme of wedded bliss, he says,

> Here Love his golden shafts imploies, here lights
> His constant Lamp, and waves his purple wings,
> Reigns here and revels.

But as attractive as is such a hard-boiled explanation of literary phenomena we shall be forced, if we proceed to boil our egg still harder, to admit that important, and almost decisive, as is the linguistic element of Milton's poem, the triumph of a work like *Paradise Lost* cannot be explained as being due to a mere accumulation of words and sounds, however splendid. There must be a fusion of these ingredients, there must be form, there must be control of the material for some great conscious, or perhaps unconscious end. And if we go on to adamantize our egg to diamond-like lucidity, its scintillation will illuminate for us the shining truth that any supreme work of art is always, or almost always, the product of a great imagination, the echo of a lofty mind, of a personality or soul possessing some kind of greatness.

Of the fusion of sound and sense by means of which such a personality can portray its visions, and vitalize and give an intense significance to the meanings, this alchemy is the ultimate secret of literature, whose explanation has escaped, and will probably forever escape, all critical analysts. I have already written of the verbal music which helps Milton to hold his enchanted readers spellbound; but his charm is by no means, nor indeed principally, a matter of musical sound alone, and I will only note that the words which we use to describe this mysterious power, *spell, charm, evocation, enchantment*, are all in their origins magical terms — terms of conjuration. Does not this suggest that great poets, and above all, Milton, possess something of the power of those magicians and exorcists and wizards who, by the rhythm and collocation of wonder-working sounds, appeal, or used to appeal, to a deep or obscure element in our nature — to the rhythm of prehistoric dances, perhaps, or the singsong of charms and conjurations? These have sunk long since below the surface of our consciousness, but we still feel

Milton and His Modern Critics

them in our bones; they live almost in the pulsation of our blood, in the rhythm of our breathing.

> *Peor* and *Baalim*,
> Forsake their Temples dim,
> With that twise-batter'd god of *Palestine* . . .
> And sullen *Moloch* fled,
> Hath left in shadows dred,
> His burning Idol all of blackest hue.
> In vain with Cymbals ring,
> They call the grisly King,
> In dismal dance about the furnace blue.

When we remember lines like these, or the lines from *Lycidas* about "the great vision of the guarded Mount," and all Milton's strange litanies of exotic names, we need not wonder at Macaulay's saying that his poetry acts like an incantation, and that his words are words of enchantment.

Seventeen

Few poets except Wordsworth have told us more about themselves than Milton. First of all there are the autobiographical digressions in his prose pamphlets which are so numerous that a volume into which they have been collected runs to many pages. Moreover his poems are full of his own experience; not only passages about his blindness, his loneliness and disillusion and his love of sacred song, but leavening the *Paradise Lost*, "and colouring the whole splendid mass of thought, theology, and fancy," is Milton's own experience.

I have read a good number of books about Milton, but of them all, the sharpest impression of the strangeness and unique quality of Milton's being I have derived from the little book in which the above phrase is printed, a book written by the Cambridge-born, but Oxford-educated scholar and novelist, Miss Rose Macaulay. "Nothing that was Milton," Miss Macaulay goes on,

Milton and His Modern Critics

"nothing that had happened to Milton, throughout his dreaming, passionate and disillusioning life, but is to be found in *Paradise Lost*." Miss Macaulay mentions first of all the imaginative child, poring over Sylvester and gathering words from that poet, then the boy at school and Cambridge, collecting phrases from the classics. Then the country loveliness of his rural retreat at Horton, then Italy, his visit to Galileo and to Vallombrosa, his unhappy marriage, and his fall from the Paradise of that dream "on to the hard, disillusioning and barren earth," and his second fall into the pessimism as to the world's future which succeeded his first glorious faith in the Revolution.

"This huge, baroque, classic, romantic, Catholic, Protestant, devil-haunted, learned amusing derivative, unique fairy-tale," as Miss Macaulay describes the *Paradise Lost*, with its "wily serpent, the bustling, skirmishing, good and bad angels, the capricious and somewhat unreasonable Almighty presiding over a Ptolemaic universe of spheres within spheres ... is by turns magnificent, engaging, tragic, tedious, fantastic, and entertaining; and has throughout the queer en-

Milton and His Modern Critics

chantment of the exotic, monstrous mind which shaped it."[1]

This is indeed a slingful of adjectives to hurl at this Goliath of our literature. But Miss Macaulay possesses by collateral inheritance from the great laudator of Milton's vocabulary her rank as a mistress of epithets, and when she calls the mind of Milton "exotic" and "monstrous" she is, to my seeming, justified in her daring.

Milton is certainly the strangest of portents, an historical problem, a literary enigma. Something unique, unheard of, "a Phoenix gazed by all," he appears from the time he left St. Paul's School "as scholarly, as accomplished and as handsome a youth as that school had ever sent forth," through his residence at Cambridge, where his delicate beauty, the peculiar grace of his appearance, brought ridicule on him, though something fierce in his nature as well as his power of fence caused him to be feared and hated. His arrogance, too, made him unpopular, and the haughty fastidiousness of his taste in morals, his

[1] *John Milton*, by Rose Macaulay. Harper & Brothers, New York and London, 1933. Printed in the United States of America, pp. 128–29.

Milton and His Modern Critics

bright virtue and "young virginity of righteousness." Castigated, was he? Well, they thought this truculent Sir Galahad deserved it; and he did deserve reprehension when he began to pour out so furious a flood of vituperation on the "canary-sucking, swan-eating" English prelates. Reprehension, too, for the way he behaved to the young girl he married, and, at the end of his life, his treatment of his neglected daughters.

But what some readers find most difficult to forgive is the Biblical narrowness of the later Milton; the disdain of the Greek philosophers, for instance, which he puts into Christ's answer to Satan when he praised them; the preference which Christ expresses for the hymns of Israel; Sion's songs being, he declares, to all true tastes so far superior to the Muses' songs that the latter might be no more, he suggests, than imperfect copies of originals in Hebrew.

Yet when at last all Milton's hopes had vanished, and as a desolate widower, impoverished and deserted by his dull daughters, "the blind old schoolmaster," as Hazlitt called him, was regarded as an infamous outcast, a republican and a regicide who had with too great clemency been

Milton and His Modern Critics

left unhanged — even from the hand of Ezra Pound, I think, must fall the whip. Especially when we see him, as Dr. Johnson describes the old poet, "in a small house, neatly enough dressed in black cloaths, sitting in a room hung with rusty green; pale but not cadaverous, with chalkstones in his hands. He said that if it were not for his gout, his blindness would be tolerable."

His mind, stored as it was with immense learning and an unequaled treasure of splendid words, was never that of a philosopher, an historian, or of a religious mystic; it is not, as Carlyle said of Dante's mind, "a large Catholic mind; rather a narrow, and even sectarian mind. . . . His greatness has, in all senses, concentred itself into fiery emphasis and depth. He is world-great not because he is world-wide, but because he is world-deep."

Of the sublimity of his mind, however, — for he is with Aeschylus among the sublimest of all poets, — of his tremendous imagination, of the sense of overpowering beauty his great poems produce, and of the potency of his vast name, there can be no question as long as there remain any readers who are sensitive to the grandeur and the loveliness of poetic sound.

Eighteen

But will the future be peopled by such readers? Who can say? Perhaps this Prince of Language will be finally driven from his word-palace, to remain with other disthroned potentates in exile forever. Perhaps the *Paradise Lost,* for which he was paid ten pounds ("Too much, too much!" they cry in Cambridge), will join Sylvester's "Du Bartas," Cowley's *Davideis,* Prior's *Solomon,* Addison's *Cato,* in the limbo of the unreadable great. Certainly the newest push of pushful Communist versifiers have not, as far as I know, ever mentioned this epic. Too busy perhaps with the study of their master Marx, they may have never heard the name of Milton mentioned.

I remember once hearing that veteran journalist, Bernard Shaw, say that any writer who had to spend more than thirty seconds to find the word he wanted should certainly give up writing. If such persons are to sit in the high seats of learning, as seems likely, this will probably be one of the rules that they will most rigorously enforce.

Milton and His Modern Critics

But perhaps such disparagers of fine writing will come to be considered (as Dr. Johnson said of the disparagers of Milton) "not as nice, but as dull," who should, he adds in a curiously modern phrase, "be pitied for their want of sensibility."

Personally I don't believe that those who take no interest in the art of words will triumph in the end. The whole history of literature seems to show that words survive in the oddest fashion the uses they are put to; one burning question burns itself out, and then another; one crisis is forgotten as a second follows, and we come to read the most earnest prophets for their style.[1] For words, as Hazlitt said, "are the only things that last forever; they are more durable than the eternal hills. Things are a mere mockery to the understanding." "Bodies, actions moulder away or melt with a sound into thin air." "By words," Sir Walter Raleigh wrote, "the world was shaped out of chaos. By words the Christian religion was established among mankind."

---

[1] "Such is the common lot of preachers and moralists. It has happened to Ecclesiastes and Isaiah and Plato, to Dante and Donne, to Bunyan and Jeremy Taylor. It is simply that men's feelings about beauty are more vital than their theories about good." (F. L. Lucas, *Studies French and English*, p. 49.)

Milton and His Modern Critics

"Weep no more" are the fitting and final words with which to address the lovers of Milton's lovely verse:—

> Weep no more, woful Shepherds weep no more,
> For *Lycidas* your sorrow is not dead,
> Sunk though he be beneath the watry floar,
> So sinks the day-star in the Ocean bed,
> And yet anon repairs his drooping head,
> And tricks his beams, and with new-spangled Ore,
> Flames in the forehead of the morning sky.

Now Lycidas the Shepherds weep no more — at least one of them doesn't. And if, as he reads Milton, his eyes are dimmed (as sometimes happens), the cause of this will not be any dread that the modern criticasters may shove the immortal poet from his throne. It will be due to the poignant beauty of this verse. Such literate expressions will be "tears of the purest moan," to borrow Milton's phrase, or, as they were described by one of his contemporaries,

> Sententious showres: O let them fall,
> Their cadence is rhetoricall.

4-1-69
on BK